Original title:
Citrus Fields Forever

Copyright © 2025 Creative Arts Management OÜ
All rights reserved.

Author: Juliana Wentworth
ISBN HARDBACK: 978-1-80586-420-2
ISBN PAPERBACK: 978-1-80586-892-7

Aromas in the Breeze

Lemon drops fall like little jokes,
Oranges giggle, and laughter chokes.
Grapefruit wears a bright new hat,
While limes play tag with the nearest cat.

Sunshine dances on a zesty tree,
Whispers of zest—just let it be!
Pineapple comes in with a grin so wide,
Making lemonade from the joy inside.

Radiant Peel

Peeling skin brings laughter loud,
As citrus fruit joins the happy crowd.
Mandarins roll like a playful ball,
While juice splashes high—we're bound to fall!

Oranges exchange their sunny winks,
Hilarity blooms as the orchard thinks.
With every bite, a funny surprise,
Juicy punchlines that light up our eyes.

Orchard's Embrace

In the grove, the fruits all hug,
Poking fun, like a friendly bug.
Limes crack jokes about their sour face,
While lemons dance with delightful grace.

Tangerines roll and play tag with glee,
Twisting and turning—look at me!
Each branch sways with laughter's delight,
In this fruity realm, all feels just right.

Blossoms in the Breeze

With blossoms giggling on every tree,
Jokes like pollen float wild and free.
Bees buzz by with a sweet little tune,
Creating a buzz of a comical boon.

The sun sneaks in with a warm embrace,
Tickling the fruits, giving each a place.
Citrus scents mix, a fragrant parade,
In this orchard laugh-fest, worries do fade.

The Secret of the Grove

In a grove where fruits are bright,
Lemons chat under the light,
Oranges dance with a silly sway,
Grapefruits giggle all day.

A secret potion made of zest,
Tickles noses, it's the best!
Mandarins serve tea with flair,
While limes complain life's not fair.

Bouncing berries join the fun,
Making merry 'til they run,
In this grove, it's pure delight,
Where laughs echo through the night.

So if you wander near this place,
Seek the fruits with grinning face,
It's a party, all agree,
In the grove of jolly glee!

Enchanted Zest

In a land where lemons gleam,
Limes play tricks with a scheme,
Tangerines sing silly songs,
While grapefruit prances along.

A wizard made of orange peel,
Mixes potions with great zeal,
Hilarity spreads with each sip,
As fruits decide to do a flip.

Chasing butterflies on a breeze,
They invent jokes with such ease,
Every laugh brings out the zest,
For in this grove, it's never rest!

When twilight casts its golden glow,
Fruits unite for the best show,
With punchlines tossed like flying pies,
Their humor shines beneath the skies!

The Golden Hour's Glow

In a land where lemons laugh and play,
Sunshine spills its golden ray.
Mandarins dance in the sunny breeze,
While oranges giggle from the trees.

The shadows stretch, the laughter grows,
Lime-green jokes in vibrant rows.
Fruits telling tales, a comedic thrill,
Makes you chuckle, sip your chill.

Breeze Through Branches

A zephyr whispers through the grove,
Tickling leaves, oh how they wove.
Lemons chat in puffed-up tones,
While grapefruits send those funny phones.

The branches sway with silly grins,
Jokes exchanged where laughter spins.
In this orchard, time stands still,
Every breeze brings a joyful thrill.

Memories of Marmalade

Oh, the sticky tales of sweet delight,
Jars of laughter shining bright.
Singing spoons with jam so grand,
Fruits unite in a gooey band.

Butterfly kisses, syrupy fun,
Breakfast giggles every one.
In every spread, a smile's found,
Marmalade magic all around.

Harvesting Happiness

With baskets full and hearts so light,
We gather joy with all our might.
Each fruit a treasure, each grin a score,
Laughter ripens, who could ask for more?

Picking oranges, we sing a tune,
Underneath the smiling moon.
Happiness spills from every bite,
Harvesting joy feels just right.

Sunlit Grove Whispers

In the grove where laughter sings,
Oranges giggle on leafy springs.
Lemons roll like pranksters bold,
Whispers of zest in stories told.

Squirrels munch on golden pies,
Underneath the sunny skies.
A bee hums tunes of sweet delight,
With every buzz, the fruits take flight.

Tangy Dreams at Dusk

As shadows stretch and daylight fades,
Limes dance in their evening parades.
Frogs croak jokes from clover beds,
While dreams of citrus dance in heads.

Grapefruits waltz 'neath the pale moon,
Their laughter echoes, a merry tune.
The crickets chirp, a playful rhyme,
In tangy dreams, we lose all time.

The Zest of Morning Light

Morning breaks with a cheerful grin,
As oranges wink, let the fun begin!
Juicy jests are tossed around,
Zesty giggles all abound.

Bananas slip on dew-kissed grass,
Limes roll by with a cheeky sass.
In this bright and silly place,
Every fruit wears a smiling face.

Orchard Serenade

With a banjo strum, the apples sway,
Singing silly songs all day.
Cherries blush with a joker's flair,
Tickling pears with a fruity air.

Under the sun, a merry crew,
Fruits unite for a lively brew.
Banquets of laughter, full of cheer,
Join the orchard, your friends are near.

Nectar of the Sunlit Harvest

The orange trees giggle, swaying with glee,
As bees wear tiny hats, buzzing with tea.
Lemons play hopscotch, dancing in rows,
While limes tell tall tales that nobody knows.

The sun pours its laughter, a bright golden stream,
Mangoes in masquerade, living the dream.
Cherries throw parties with zest in the air,
A fruity confetti, a tropical flair.

Shadows in the Lemon Grove

Lemonade glasses wearing shades of delight,
As oranges play poker late into the night.
The lime cousins argue, who's zestier still,
While grapefruits roll dice, claiming their thrill.

In shadows of green, laughter echoes on,
With fruit flies in bowties, strutting till dawn.
Bananas in pajamas dance round and round,
As the sun keeps on shining, joyfully unbound.

A Dance of Citrus Dreams

Waltzing under branches, they spin and sway,
Fruit bowls gossiping, come join the ballet!
A clementine twirls in its peel so bright,
While strawberries giggle, oh what a sight!

The party continues as night turns to day,
With fruitcake fantasies, come join the fray.
Tangerines juggle, a talented crew,
In this zesty parade, there's always room for you.

The Taste of Sun-Kissed Joy

Lemon puns bubble up in the summer heat,
With every slice shared, there's fun to repeat.
Grapefruit grins wide, chattering so fast,
As pear plays the comedian, laughter amassed.

The tangy aroma, mixed with pure cheer,
As oranges dare each other to dance near.
Under the sun, every fruit's a delight,
In this juicy carnival, the mood is just right.

Citrus Breeze Reverie

In a grove where laughter grows,
Oranges dance on tippy toes.
Lemons chuckle, their zest quite bright,
Grapefruits grin, a silly sight.

A squirrel slipped, what a sight to see,
Chasing fruit like it's a spree.
With every peel, a giggle bursts,
In this land, joy really thirsts.

Golden Slices of Dawn

Morning smiles with a tangy flair,
Breakfast toast with a fruity scare.
Butterflies sip on nectar sweet,
While bees buzz and shuffle their feet.

Marmalade slips like a slippery clown,
Stealing the show with a sugary crown.
Orange juice drips with cheeky glee,
Filling our cups just like a spree.

The Aroma of Abundance

Fragrant scents waft, oh what a tease,
Limes laughing, and lemons sneeze.
In this orchard, the harvest sings,
With each fruit comes a giggle that clings.

Jars of jam line up in a row,
Wobbly jars, they steal the show.
Slip on a peel, what a surprise,
Rolling in laughter, oh how time flies!

Harvest Moon

Under the glow of a quirky moon,
Citrus critters dance to a silly tune.
Tangerines twirl with orange delight,
While grapefruits leap, what a funny sight!

Fields aglow with a yellow hue,
Mice breakdance, they're feeling new.
Stars chuckle as fruit falls down,
The harvest party wears a clown's crown.

Sweet Sunlight

Sunbeams play with the bumpy fruit,
Lemonade rivers, oh what a hoot!
Under the sun, oranges have fun,
Basking in laughter, they splish and run.

Chickens cluck at a juicy snack,
Peeling back smiles, no laughter they lack.
As ray by ray, they roll and spin,
In this bright world, let the fun begin!

Fragrant Paths of Orange

In orange groves where laughter grows,
The fruit hangs low, the sweetness shows.
A squirrel spins tales of juicy delight,
While birds make a chorus, taking flight.

Juggling oranges with joy, we stand,
But one slips away, it rolls from our hand.
A chase ensues, the fruit takes a lead,
We stumble and giggle, it's all that we need.

Lush Canopy Melodies

Under leafy boughs where shadows dance,
We hum to the tunes of our citrus romance.
A whiff of zest brings smiles that bloom,
And then we find a frog in bloom!

He croaks a tune to the fluttering bees,
While ants march along, doing as they please.
Each branch a stage for this woodland show,
We laugh 'til we snort, in the sun's warm glow.

Secrets of the Lemon Orchard

In a grove where lemons whisper sweet,
We plan a prank with zestful feat.
A lemon's pranked a curious hare,
He sniffs and hops; he's caught unaware!

With lemonade dreams and silliness near,
We trample the turf, chased by the deer.
Frolicking laughter, oh what a sight!
As we squeeze out fun under the light.

Ripe Citrus Symphony

A grand orchestra of citrus delight,
With oranges plucking strings under the light.
Lemons play horns, all shiny and bright,
As limes join in for the ultimate fight!

The audience giggles, too giddy to clap,
As grapefruits tumble right into our lap.
The conductor's a parrot, squawking with flair,
We're caught in the music, no worries, no care.

Lush Labyrinth

In a grove where oranges dance,
Lemons play a silly prance,
Tangerines wear hats so bright,
Grapefruits giggle in the light.

A squirrel juggles juicy lime,
While birds hum a fruity rhyme,
Bees with shades buzz here and there,
Riding on a fragrant air.

Each twist and turn a zesty spree,
With whispers from the orange tree,
Laughter spills like sunlit dew,
As fruit flies join the party too.

So skip along this juicy maze,
Where nature's humor sings in rays,
And every step's a tasty joke,
In this land where sunshine stokes.

The Magic of Marigold

In gardens where the wild things bloom,
Marigolds create a funny room,
Chasing shadows with a flair,
Jokes are tossed up in the air.

A parrot mimics with delight,
As gnomes discuss the day's first light,
With petals bright, they share a grin,
In marigolds, the laughs begin.

A bumblebee in fancy shoes,
Dances 'round like it's got the blues,
While butterflies all join the fun,
Sipping nectar 'til they're done.

And as the sun begins to fade,
The flowers laugh, a soft brigade,
In this magic where joy enfolds,
Every petal has a story told.

Fragrant Footprints

Down a path of scent and cheer,
Footprints lead to laughter near,
Mint and basil spill their jokes,
While thyme pokes fun at coriander folks.

Chives recite their punchline tales,
As garlic winks and softly hails,
Rosemary rolls in a fit of glee,
Sage laughs hard, can't you see?

A walk through herbs, a fragrant dance,
Each leaf a player in this prance,
With every step a giggle grows,
In the garden where humor flows.

So wander among the spicy mirth,
In this place that knows no dearth,
With fragrant footprints, joy arrived,
In fields of laughter, we're alive.

Evergreen Euphoria

Amongst the pines that twist and twine,
Where evergreens in jest recline,
A squirrel sports a tree-top cap,
While laugh tracks play in nature's lap.

Beneath the branches, shadows play,
As pine cones throw their jokes all day,
The air's a punchline, crisp and clear,
Laughter mingles with the cheer.

A chipmunk's chuckle fills the air,
As nature's humor finds a spare,
Spruce and fir join in a dance,
Leaving us caught in their romance.

So bask beneath the broadleaf skies,
In evergreen where mirth complies,
In this happy, leafy spree,
Life's funnier than it seems to be.

Sunlit Canopies

Under branches, lemons sway,
A squirrel's trying to steal a bouquet.
Orange dreams in laughter burst,
A fruity joke, we can't be cursed.

Bees take tango on a rim,
Juggling nectar on a whim.
Sunshine giggles, shadows play,
Here's to zest, hip-hip-Hooray!

The Freshness of Dawn

Morning breaks with citrus cheer,
I dread the thought of waking near.
Juicy laughter fills the air,
A zestful start beyond compare.

Lemonade dreams on toast so bright,
Who knew that zest could bring such light?
Wake up, world, no time to yawn,
Let's squeeze the day, come on, come on!

Zesty Wanderlust

Pack your bags with limes and zest,
A fruity road trip sounds the best!
Tangerine sun with shades of glee,
Join me, friend, let's roam carefree!

Lemon trees wave on the route,
The aroma's something to shout about.
Each stop we make is a sweet delight,
Why not dance under streetlight?

The Peel of Daybreak

Awake to peels that greet the sun,
Banana split, oh what fun!
Morning tang is a jolly tune,
Let's make the kitchen our cartoon.

Slice and dice with laughter's flair,
Orange juice spills, we just don't care!
Tickling tongues and juicy smiles,
In our orchard, let's stay awhile!

Zestful Reckoning

In a grove where oranges roll,
Lemons giggle, playing their role.
Limes declare, 'We're here for fun!'
While grapefruits bask in the sun.

Pickers dance with fruited bliss,
Slipping on a juicy kiss.
A tangerine takes a bold dash,
Leaving behind a vibrant splash.

Sour faces turn to glee,
As they squeeze juice like it's free.
'What a twist!' cry all the fruits,
As squirrels join in, wearing suits.

A fruitcake dreams outside its box,
Swings high from a tree with shocks.
In this grove, it's all in jest,
Where every bite is quite the zest!

The Tangy Tapestry

In colors bright, the fruits unite,
Dancing daily, bringing light.
Lemonade rivers freely flow,
While fruit flies put on a show.

"Juice us up!' the berries sing,
As grapefruits bounce with bouncing bling.
A citrus party, never dull,
With jokes and puns, they pull and pull.

Chasing each other round the bend,
An orange yells, 'Let's not pretend!'
A peel slips, laughter fills the air,
A zesty scene beyond compare.

Underneath the laughing trees,
Every breeze is thick with tease.
In this world of tangy cheer,
Each day's a fruit-filled souvenir!

Lush Citrus Horizon

Across the vista, colors gleam,
Lemon lights up like a dream.
Oranges roller-skate around,
While figs get tangled on the ground.

Grapefruits race, it's quite a sight,
Chasing each other, day and night.
Their peels are like a wild disguise,
With citrus masks, they strategize.

In each crevice, laughter blooms,
As fruits gather in making rooms.
Silly games of 'Catch the Juice'
Set the grove alive, let loose!

Under the sun, all try to compete,
But in this grove, all find their seat.
With each bite, a smile we earn,
In this horizon, bright and fun to churn!

Encounters in the Grove

Underneath the leafy bowers,
Fruits gather for their happy hours.
Oranges brag, claiming they're best,
While lemons roll in, dressed for the fest.

A comet made of fruit peels flies,
Laughing loudly, offering pies.
Beneath the branches, tales unfold,
As zestful secrets, untold gold.

With pranks afoot, the fruits collide,
Grapes giggle, 'Let's take a ride!'
Ripe mischief, served with a twist,
Not a chance for the gloom to exist!

As sunset paints the sky so bright,
Citrus giggles in delight.
In this grove, laughter prevails,
With fruity friends and zesty tales.

Echoes of Juicy Laughter

In a grove where lemons play,
Oranges dance throughout the day,
Limes wear hats that are too big,
They're all on a ridiculous jig.

Grapefruits giggle, bouncing round,
With zestful whispers, joy is found,
Chasing bees who tell a joke,
While laughing trees begin to choke.

Tangerines toss quips with flair,
They throw their peels without a care,
The fruity choir shouts with glee,
As laughter echoes through the spree.

So grab your friends and join the cheer,
In this orchard, fun's the premiere,
A slippery path of playful schemes,
Where humor grows in sunlit beams.

Citrus Moonlight

Underneath the silver glow,
A lemon cast a shadow show,
The oranges sang a silly tune,
While clementines danced to the moon.

Limes were laughing, rolling fast,
In their zesty games, none could last,
Grapefruits juggled in a zest,
Declaring that juiciness is best.

With moonlit jokes and goofy ways,
They brighten up the dullest days,
A merry band of fruity friends,
Their chuckles echo, never ends.

So join the party, take a spin,
Where mirth and sweetness surely win,
In this land of light and cheer,
Where laughs are ripe, and joy is near.

Embrace of the Orchard

In the warmth of morning's kiss,
Oranges roll with fruity bliss,
Lemon trees wear silly hats,
As laughter bounces like chitchats.

Bumbling bees on quirky quests,
Join the fun, they're dressed the best,
With nectar dreams, they zoom and zip,
Through branches, they joyously skip.

Bananas slip, but never frown,
While tangerines spin round and round,
With the sun in a golden frame,
This orchard's wild, a playful game.

Peeling laughter, zest in the air,
With every joke, shed not a care,
So gather all, come laugh and blend,
In this orchard, where dreams transcend.

Elysian Citrus

In a garden where giggles thrive,
Bright fruits unite to feel alive,
Limes and lemons blend their cheer,
Ripe with humor, they persevere.

Their laughter bubbles, sweetly spun,
As oranges frolic in the sun,
Twirling peels like confetti bright,
In a party that feels just right.

Grapefruits prance in merry lines,
Telling tales with fruity vines,
With every punchline, joy does sprout,
In this play where fun's about.

So rally friends, with zestful hearts,
Join the fun, where laughter starts,
In this land of playful cheer,
Where every moment shines so clear.

Melody of the Grove

In the grove, a lemon sings,
Doing flips with happy wings.
Oranges dance in pairs so bright,
Jiving under the moonlight.

Limes are laughing, what a scene,
Poking fun at tangerine.
Grapefruits roll with laughter's glee,
As they spill their zestful spree.

A wacky band of fruit so bold,
Strumming tunes of sweet and cold.
This orchard's got a comic charm,
Where every fruit's a different harm.

So let's break out the joyful cheer,
In the grove, we have no fear.
With every squeeze and twist we make,
We celebrate the fruitcake break!

The Last Drop of Summer

The sun is hot, the squeeze is tight,
Juicy shenanigans take flight.
Lemonade flows in rivers wide,
While ice cream trucks in chaos glide.

Watermelons toss like balls,
As we dodge the summer squalls.
A splash of juice, a sticky hand,
We're all part of this fruit stand.

Pickled oranges in a jam,
Thinking they're the ultimate slam.
But cherries steal the funky show,
With giggles as their juices flow.

Let's take a sip of sunny cheer,
As summer's last drop rolls near.
A toast to juiciness galore,
Don't let this harvest be a bore!

Essence of Earth

In patches green, the fruits collide,
With wobbly dances filled with pride.
Mangoes giggle, bouncing high,
While blueberries whisper, "Let's all fly!"

Pineapples wear their crowns just right,
Poking fun in the broad daylight.
Bananas slip on jokes of old,
In this land where zest is gold.

Ripe avocados strike a pose,
As their creamy dreams compose.
While kiwi joins the grassy play,
Spinning tales of summer's sway.

Essence of joy in every bite,
Bringing laughter, pure delight.
A fruit parade, all colors sing,
In harmony, the orchard swings!

Sunset over the Orchard

The sun dips low, a ball of fire,
As fruit-hats bob and dreams inspire.
Grapes do tricks, they roll and hop,
As shadows stretch and daylight stops.

The orange sky ignites the fun,
With fruity pranks for everyone.
Lemon clouds float by, so sweet,
While laughing fruits dance on their feet.

Peaches share the last warm light,
In the orchard, it feels so right.
A sunset play, with zest and cheer,
As nature laughs, we all draw near.

So raise a glass to twilight's call,
In this orchard, we'll have a ball.
With every shade the day shall keep,
Let fruity dreams, forever leap!

Grove Guardians

In the orchard where we stand,
Lemons giggle at our hands.
Oranges roll and laugh with glee,
Kiwi wears a hat, just for me.

Silly squirrels dance around,
In this place where joy is found.
Grapefruits wink, oh what a sight,
The garden party lasts all night.

Lime slices join the playful fray,
Mangoes cheer, 'Hip, hip, hooray!'
We're the protectors, brave and bold,
Keeping secrets of fruit untold.

With our laughter, fruit takes flight,
In the grove, we feel so bright.
Who knew orchards could be this fun?
Join our antics, everyone!

The Tickle of Tang

A twist in every juicy bite,
Oranges make the morning bright.
Lemonade laughs with a punch,
Citrusy jokes for every brunch.

Pickled peels on a sunny day,
Sour and sweet come out to play.
Grapefruit hats on dapper birds,
Whisper wild and wacky words.

In every squeeze, a giggle hides,
Tangerines roll in silly rides.
Fruits unite and tease today,
Join the dance; don't be so gray!

Pineapples wear a crown of glee,
Spinning tales of jubilee.
Lemon trees join in the fun,
Under the rays of the warming sun.

Sunbeam Harvest

Golden rays upon the skin,
Fruit-filled laughter blows in wind.
Sunflowers cheer as we do roam,
Under this fruity, sunny dome.

Bouncing berries roll and dive,
In the heat, we come alive.
Peaches blush while lemons sing,
In this place, we're all a fling.

Harvest's here; let's make a toast,
To silly fruits we love the most.
Dancing vines with a twist,
Please don't let the harvest miss!

Moments sweet, and juice galore,
Add a giggle, never a bore.
Join the feast, the fun's begun,
Life's too short; let's run, run, run!

Zestful Independence

Freedom rings in every zest,
Fruits declare their fun-filled fest.
Squirrels shake with citrus cheer,
Celebrating life without any fear.

Lime grenades in silly toss,
Lemon lives, we can't be lost.
Tangerine twirls on the breeze,
Keeping our spirits at ease.

With every slice, our giggles rise,
In this land of sweet surprise.
Juicy dreams, we dare to chase,
Living life with zest and grace.

Together we'll burst into laughter,
Savoring joy, here and after.
So grab a fruit, don't hesitate,
Join our party; it's never too late!

Juxtaposed Juices

In a land where lemons laugh,
Limes dance in silly socks,
Oranges juggle fruits and halves,
While grapefruits wear fancy frocks.

Lemonade spills a funny tale,
As melons float in teacups wide,
Tangy giggles never fail,
To brighten up a sunny ride.

With every sip a joke is told,
Peeling laughter from the trees,
In this world of sweet and bold,
Juices blend as they please.

So raise your glass, toast to the cheer,
Quirky flavors all around,
In this fruity kingdom dear,
Silly sips of joy abound!

Honeyed Evenings

As night descends, the fruits awake,
Grapes in pajamas, ready to chat,
Oranges boast of the juice they make,
While lemons giggle, "Have a seat, fat cat!"

Fireflies dance in the twilight glow,
Fruits are mixing drinks in a bowl,
Bumbling bees buzz to and fro,
Sweet honeyed laughter fills the soul.

Cherries play tag around the fence,
Strawberries slip on a silky slide,
Peaches take turns, feeling immense,
In this orchard where joys collide.

So cheers to nights of fruity delight,
Where laughter sparkles with each sip,
May honeyed moments take flight,
On this enchanting, joyous trip!

Citrus Cascade

A waterfall of zest appears,
Lemons plunge in a fizzy dive,
Lime slices fly like funny spears,
In this splash where fruits come alive.

Grapefruits slide with a cheeky grin,
While oranges flip with flair and might,
Pineapples chuckle, ready to spin,
As juice rains down with pure delight.

Tangerines pirouette with glee,
Kiwis bounce on a citrus wave,
Bananas play peek-a-boo with me,
In this fruity plunge, we all behave.

So join the splash, don't be shy,
Let the colors swirl and blend,
With each twist, we laugh and fly,
In a cascade that never ends!

A Chorus of Colors

A chorus sings in hues so bright,
Mangoes hum a sunny tune,
Limes join in with pure delight,
As tangerines sway 'neath the moon.

A grapefruit belts a jazzy note,
With lemons tapping in the back,
Peaches sway like they're on a boat,
In this fruity, vibrant pack.

Cherries harmonize a sweet refrain,
As nectarines twirl on the stage,
Kiwis giggle in the rain,
In this fruity fest, we engage.

So gather 'round, let's start the cheer,
For this fruity band won't wane,
In colors bold, the joys appear,
A chorus shared, we'll never feign!

The Sweetness of Ripeness

In the sun, they dangle bright,
Juicy treasures, pure delight.
A squirrel sniffs, then takes a leap,
Dreaming of the fruit to keep.

Lemonade stands and sticky hands,
We dance with fruit, in merry bands.
A rogue orange rolls away,
We chase it down—what a display!

Limes laugh loud, they wear their zest,
Juggling juiciness, they're the best.
With every slice, a giggle bursts,
From tart to sweet, we quench our thirst!

So here's to fruits that brighten days,
In every squeeze, a funny phase.
With every bite, a joy unfolds,
These fruits of laughter, pure as gold.

A Symphony of Slices

In a kitchen, chaos reigns,
Slicing fruits brings silly pains.
Oranges spin; oh what a sight,
Lemon wedges take to flight!

A tangerine has gone astray,
It rolled off the counter; what a play!
Citrusy notes fill the air,
As giggles rise, a fruity affair!

A melon drops with a loud thud,
Making splashes like a flood.
In a bowl, a wacky dance,
As fruits collide, they dare to prance!

The blender hums a zesty tune,
As juice erupts like a cartoon!
Sipping flavors, smiles wide,
In our fruity world, we take pride.

Limoncello Lullabies

In the night, a sweet delight,
A limoncello dreams take flight.
Under stars, we swirl and sing,
As laughter flows from every fling.

Zesty notes in every sip,
As we waltz and take a dip.
Cool breeze carries playful cheers,
With every slice, we conquer fears!

Lemons dance with giddy flair,
In a jug, they fill the air.
Sipping slow, our giggles meld,
In shining glasses, joy is held!

With citrus tunes that softly ring,
We toast to life and everything.
In every drop, sweet memories stay,
A lullaby that's here to play.

Grove of Gold

In orchards bright with golden hue,
A world of laughs, with zest anew.
Where every tree a joke can tell,
In the grove, we laugh so well!

Lemon peels, a slippery track,
Orange jokes keep coming back.
With every bite, a pun takes flight,
In this grove, it's pure delight!

Twirling fruits like tops, oh dear,
A merry band of citrus cheer.
Underneath the sun's warm spell,
The grove enchants with every smell!

With friends beside, we share the fun,
In laughter, juice, we come undone.
A citrus patch of golden dreams,
We raise our glasses, bursting seams!

Citrus Reverie

In a grove of orange glee,
Lemons danced with jubilee.
A grapefruit told a silly joke,
While tangerines laughed till they broke.

The limes rolled out a zesty cheer,
Each fruit giggled, spread good cheer.
Mandarins in a fancy parade,
All wore hats, none were afraid.

A splash of juice, a burst of zest,
In this orchard, life's the best.
Chasing butterflies, oh what fun,
Under the bright, warm sun.

So here we sing, so here we play,
In this land where citrus stay.
With each slice, a smile anew,
In our citrusy rendezvous.

Tangy Trails

Down the roads of yellow hue,
Lemons lead a comedic crew.
They tripped on peels, rolled with laughter,
Chasing dreams, and silly banter.

A lime slipped and lost its hat,
A bumpkin giggle, just like that.
In this orchard, fun's no grind,
Fruit on the move, and never blind.

Tangerines juggled in a row,
While oranges danced, putting on a show.
With every hop, a punchline lands,
In these tangy, cheerful lands.

So join the zest and bring a grin,
Where laughter's ripe, let's all begin.
A track of fun, where joy prevails,
Through our delightful tangy trails.

Harvest Moon's Glow

Beneath the moon, what a sight!
Fruits had a party, oh what delight!
Juggling stars, a lime-lamp glow,
Orange balloons floating to and fro.

Lemons yelled, "Make room and dance!
Let's give this night a silly chance!"
The grapefruits rolled and joined the jam,
Each color shining, just like a slam.

"Mondays are tough!" the oranges cried,
"Let's twist and twirl, let's not subside!"
Under the harvest's brilliant blaze,
In goofy ways, our hearts we'd raise.

So toast the night with fruit punch cheer,
As harvest moons draw friends near.
With giggles loud, we'll steal the show,
In the glow of the moon's soft glow.

In the Shade of Oranges

In the shade of fruit so bright,
Laughter bubbles, pure delight.
Lemonade stands up to tease,
As giggles echo on the breeze.

A squirrel popped in, nose in the air,
"Got any snacks? A snack to share?"
Oranges rolled, they tossed and played,
In this orchard, joy displayed.

Tangerine tea parties, oh so grand,
With strawberry cookies, snacks on hand.
Sipping juice, the fun won't cease,
In this quirky, fruity peace.

So have a laugh, forget the strife,
Join our jolly citrus life.
Under the shade, we'll sing and sway,
In this orchard where we'll stay.

Limoncello Twilight Fancy

In twilight's grasp, a lemon dance,
With every sip, the worlds enhance.
A twist of fate, a splash of cheer,
Limoncello dreams, let's pour a beer.

A pizza slice all draped in zest,
On sunny days, we're at our best.
Each sticky laugh, a sweet reprise,
As citrus pranks float through the skies.

A skit of oranges, they take the stage,
In hats and ties, they're all the rage.
They juggle limes while cracking jokes,
In this grand show, the fruit awokes.

So raise your glass, let laughter race,
For every drop could win a place.
In limoncello twilight's embrace,
We'll dance and twirl, oh what a chase!

Echoes of Tangerine Sunsets

The tangerine laughs in the glowing night,
With every wink, they bring delight.
Purple skies and citrus dreams,
In fruit stand fairy tales, nothing's as it seems.

Chasing shadows that skip and roll,
Oranges in capes, they're on a stroll.
They bicker over who's the king,
With peel to peel, they shout and sing.

The sunset draped in orange glow,
As fruit-flavored fireworks start to flow.
Each burst of zest, a comic plight,
Tangerine echoes dance in flight.

So let's toast to this fruity crew,
Their zest-filled lives—who needs a zoo?
As shadows blend in sunset charms,
We'll laugh along and share our charms!

Zestful Dreams

In dreams that twirl with zest and spice,
Sweet oranges debate just once or twice.
They wear cool shades, take sunlit strolls,
With laughter echoing from their souls.

A twist of lime runs for a chair,
While grapefruit jokes hang in the air.
They giggle hard, then roll around,
In zestful dreams, pure joy is found.

In lemonade fairs, we eat the pie,
As fruit debates what dreams can fly.
Squishy berries join in too,
Tasting the world with a splashy crew.

So let's dive deep and sip the fun,
In zestful dreams, we've only begun.
With every laugh, we'll burst and gleam,
Join this parade—let's live the dream!

Orchard Whispers

In orchards wide, the whispers float,
With tangy tales, they all devote.
A lemon wiggles, the lime's a thief,
Stealing glances, they laugh with relief.

The grapefruits gossip with juicy flair,
While kiwis plot some wild affair.
They dream of dances in starlit nights,
Trading jokes in fruit-laden flights.

Ripe peaches blushing, oh what a sight,
Share giggles backstage, sparkling bright.
With every bite, they steal the show,
In orchard whispers, the laughter's aglow.

So gather 'round, let spirits soar,
As fruits unite, can't ask for more.
With glimmers of this playful spree,
Orchard whispers, where we're all free!

Fields of Flavor

In the orchard, squishy feet,
Lemon drops, a tangy treat.
Oranges roll, a bouncing game,
Grapefruit giggles, who's to blame?

Sour faces, kids in fright,
Juice wars start; what a sight!
Citrus chaos fills the air,
When one slips, we all will share!

Limeade splashes, sticky hands,
Lemonade stands, wobbly stands.
In this patch of zesty glee,
We laugh as sweet as honeybee!

Sunshine smiles on every tree,
Funny hats for you and me.
Nature's joy, bright hues combined,
In these fields, we're citrus-twined.

Juicy Daydream

Beneath the sun, a gleeful sway,
Lemons dance, they shout hooray!
Tangerine twirls in the breeze,
While oranges play hide-and-seek with trees.

In a dream of citrus cheer,
The fruit parade draws near!
Kooky lemon guards the gate,
Time to munch, but wait, don't wait!

Citrus capers on parade,
Grapefruit's here, costume made!
Funky hats and juicy shoes,
Stepping to the fruity blues!

In this dreamy, zesty land,
We laugh till we can't stand.
With each squeeze, a burst of fun,
A juicy day has just begun!

Beneath the Lemon Tree

Underneath that lemon tree,
We host a sour jubilee!
Sticky fingers, funny hats,
Lemonade wars with silly spats.

Swinging high, we take a chance,
Landing soft in citrus dance.
While the bees all hum a tune,
We groove in shades of bright balloon!

Sour lemon, don't you pout,
Add some sugar, this is clout!
Wacky faces, pucker tight,
Beneath the tree, it feels just right!

With giggles bouncing on the breeze,
Juicy laughter fills the trees.
In this playful, fruity spree,
Friendship grows with every squeeze!

The Scent of Summer

The scent of summer's citrus breeze,
Funky fruits dance with ease.
Zesty snacks upon the lawn,
Wobbly kids, till dusk at dawn!

Peeled oranges rolling free,
A leap of faith—a bouncy spree!
Squirrels laugh at all our tricks,
As fruit flies try out their flicks!

Bold lemons make a grand parade,
Tart and sweet; we're unafraid.
With each squeeze, we make a wish,
For more lazy days, all delish!

In this summer's fruity cheer,
We whistle tunes for all to hear.
With smiles bright and hearts so light,
Citrus fun, from morn till night!

Radiance in Every Peel

In the orchard, laughter rings,
Where oranges dance and the lemon sings.
A grapefruit slips, oh what a sight,
As citrus critters party all night!

Tangerine dreams with a twist of delight,
While limes play tag in the pale moonlight.
With every squirt, a giggle erupts,
These fruity shenanigans, who would interrupt?

The sunbeams splash on each glowing sphere,
As juice drips down, bringing us cheer.
A zest so bright, it's hard to conceal,
In this orchard of joy, there's magic to feel!

So raise a toast with that zesty drink,
To fruit-fueled fun—don't you dare blink!
With every bite, let the good times reveal,
The radiance found in each playful peel.

Juices of Time and Memory

Under the sun where memories sprout,
Lemonade laughter spills all about.
Sipping on sunshine, what a delight,
While orange slices dance in the light.

With each sip, the past comes alive,
A zesty time-traveling hive!
Grapefruits giggle as they reminisce,
Of silly moments, we just can't miss.

The clock ticks slow as we make a toast,
To fruity friendships we cherish the most.
A dash of nostalgia, a splash of cheer,
With juices of time, we hold moments dear.

So let's squeeze joy from every last drop,
As memories bubble and never stop.
In this tangy fiesta, we'll all feel free,
With laughter and love, just you and me.

Between the Trees of Gold

Beneath the canopy where laughter grows,
Fruits in their glory, an endless show.
A playful breeze tickles the leaves,
As orange and lemon play tricks, oh please!

In a world where grapefruits giggle and leap,
We chase after zest—oh, what a heap!
Between the rows of trees, we scheme,
Plotting to catch a citrus-themed dream.

With every peel, a treasure is found,
An orchard alive with joy all around.
The laughter bubbles like soda in the air,
In this land of citrus, we banish despair.

So let's swing from branches, and dance with delight,
As the sun sets low, igniting the night.
Between the trees of gold, we all will belong,
Creating a tapestry woven with song.

Nature's Zesty Embrace

In the glow of twilight, the oranges gleam,
Nature's embrace, oh what a dream!
With fluffy clouds resembling a pie,
Laughter erupts as the lemons fly!

The tangy tunes from a nearby grove,
Invite us in, let the silliness rove.
Limes loll about, acting quite bold,
In this zesty embrace, we need to be told!

Let's twirl in the grass, where fruit-scented air
Whispers sweet secrets that we love to share.
With every giggle, the world feels alive,
In nature's embrace, we learn how to thrive.

So wear your fruit crown, don your best grin,
In this zesty romp, we all are akin.
With oranges and laughter wrapped up in grace,
Together we frolic in nature's embrace.

The Rind of Reminiscence

In sunny groves where laughter grew,
Jokes were tossed like fruit on cue.
Peels of humor, bright and bold,
Squeezed from memories, tales retold.

Citrus pranks, they filled the air,
With zestful laughs, beyond compare.
Oranges rolling, lemons' cheer,
In a world where smiles appear.

A grapefruit's grin, a tangerine's tease,
Knocking on doors, waving with ease.
Rind and revelry, a joyful dance,
In this fruity whimsy, we find our chance.

So gather 'round, let's share a squeeze,
Of citrus joy, to float with ease.
In this orchard, the laughter flows,
As we embrace the fun that grows.

Sweetened Paths

Beneath the trees, we chase our dreams,
With every bite, a giggle seems.
Lemons chuckle, limes roll tight,
In this garden, pure delight.

Soursweet tales in every twist,
Juicy moments that can't be missed.
We hop along these golden trails,
Dodging citrus as humor prevails.

A jester orange, wearing a crown,
Laughing at worries, turning frowns down.
Sweetened paths where laughter leads,
In this citrus realm, joy succeeds.

So come along, let's skip and sing,
In fields of fruit, joy takes wing.
With every chuckle, our spirits lift,
In a world where sweetness is the gift.

Citrus Dancers

Lemons twirl in skirts of zest,
Swaying dancers, oh what a fest!
Oranges frolic, grapefruits leap,
As laughter echoes, running deep.

Funky rhythms of juice and cheer,
Slicing through the atmosphere.
With every move, a pun's embrace,
Citrus dancers, a merry chase.

Lime's a joker, with a wink,
Cracking jokes as we all drink.
In this fiesta, we find our groove,
As fruits shimmy and laughter moves.

So grab your partner, don't be shy,
Join the dance beneath the sky.
In this orchard of glee we prance,
With every step, we take a chance.

Lemonade Lament

In a pitcher bright, our tales collide,
Stirring sweet memories, side by side.
A splash of laughter, a twist of fate,
Lemonade dreams we all create.

Soursweet sorrows in every sip,
Sliding down with a citrus flip.
Grapefruit woes in a shaker spun,
Turning frowns into punchlines fun.

Ice cubes clink like jokes on air,
Sipping sunshine without a care.
With every gulp, a giggle spills,
A liquid joy that gently thrills.

So raise your glass, let laughter flow,
In this lemonade, the smiles glow.
To juicy stories and moments rife,
Where every sip brings zest to life.

Lush Green Ambiance

In the grove where laughter grows,
Lemons dance in sunny shows.
Oranges giggle in the breeze,
While grapefruits plan their silly tease.

A parrot squawks a joke too loud,
As tangerines act like a crowd.
Juice drips down in a comic way,
Mimicking clowns who love to play.

Squirrels chase each other fast,
While limes poke fun at the past.
Cherry blossoms fall like rain,
Creating mischief, never pain.

With every bounce and silly cheer,
The fruits unite, as fun draws near.
In this grove, the joy is spread,
With fruity puns, they dance instead.

Shadows of Citrus

In shadows where the sunbeams play,
Limes plot jokes and tease all day.
Meyer lemons in hats so bright,
Claim they own the dance floor night.

Tangerines tell tales of woe,
About the time they lost their glow.
But then they burst with zestful glee,
Saying, "Buy one, get one free!"

The oranges join, a jolly crew,
Organizing a fruit parade too.
Watermelons laugh, their seeds in flight,
As berries cheer with all their might.

Underneath the leafy dome,
The zestful fun feels like home.
So snack a laugh or peel a grin,
In shadows where the fun begins.

Citrus Caravan

Join the zesty caravan,
Where fruits and laughter make a plan.
Lemons ride in silly peels,
As grapefruits spin on squeaky wheels.

With a trumpet sound from a juicy lime,
They roll away in fruity rhyme.
Tangerines toss confetti bright,
As the whole crew takes off in flight.

Oranges juggle with tasty flair,
While cherries dance without a care.
The watermelons sing a tune,
Beneath the smiling, shining moon.

So join this fruity, merry quest,
Where every twist is simply the best.
In every bite, a laugh awaits,
In this caravan, love translates.

Orchard of Echoes

In the orchard where echoes sing,
The fruits enjoy a playful fling.
Citrus voices bounce around,
Chasing giggles, joy is found.

Grapefruits play hide-and-seek,
Orange jokes, oh-so-unique!
Lemons laugh with zesty flair,
Creating echoes everywhere.

Underneath the branches wide,
Fruits share secrets, side by side.
With every joke and playful jest,
Their friendship puts them to the test.

So come and join this fruity spree,
In the orchard, wild and free.
With echoes of laughter filling the air,
These merry fruits beyond compare.

Blossom Kisses in the Air

In a grove where laughter grows,
Bees wear tiny hats, who knows?
Chasing pollen like it's gold,
Sweet shenanigans unfold.

Wobbly chins and sticky hands,
We dance like silly bands.
Each bloom a giggle, bright and cheery,
Nature's punchline, oh so merry.

As we twirl through fragrant trees,
The air is filled with fruit-filled breeze.
Lemons laugh, they juggle too,
Making jokes, just me and you.

Fields of Sunlit Citrus

In fields where oranges play around,
Juicy jokes are often found.
Lemons rolling in the sun,
Making jest of everyone.

A grapefruit's twist, a citrus cheer,
Squirrels giggle, never fear!
They wear bow ties and do a dance,
In this land of sweet expanse.

Lemons say, "We're the zest!"
Limes retort, "No time to rest!"
Chasing each other, round and round,
In this playful, sunny ground.

The Word of Juicy Moments

Gather 'round for fruity tales,
Where every citrus laughter sails.
A tangent of tangy delight,
As grapefruits play tag in the light.

Lime says, "I'm a funny chap!"
While oranges fall into a nap.
Juicy secrets on the vine,
Stories spun with zest and wine.

Tangerines toast with a grin,
Mischief bubbles from within.
Each squeeze brings giggles galore,
Juicy moments we explore.

The Orange Blossom Promise

In a world of playful bloom,
We toss our worries, make room.
With every breeze, a giggle flies,
A promise wrapped in sweet surprise.

A frog sings serenades at dawn,
While oranges hum along, not drawn.
"We'll never sour, just stay bright!"
In this orchard, hearts take flight.

A jester's cap on every tree,
Prancing fruit, oh, what a spree!
Kisses of blossom in the air,
Life's juiciest moments, beyond compare.

Dancing with the Sun

When morning stretches, yawns so wide,
The lemons laugh, they can't abide.
A grapefruit twirls, what a sight,
They shimmy and sway until the night.

With sandals made of zest so bright,
They prance and caper, pure delight.
The sun takes selfies, how absurd,
As fruity giggles fill the birds.

Beneath the beams, the limes engage,
In dapper hats, they set the stage.
A dance-off here, a twist and turn,
For every splash, the citrus yearn.

In this bright ball, the laughter grows,
As oranges take on fancy clothes.
With every shuffle, riotous cheer,
The sun just sighs, "I love it here!"

Oranges at Dusk

As dusk descends with a playful wink,
The oranges gather, time to think.
With little hats and tiny shoes,
They share their secrets, pick and choose.

A sunset glow hits cheeks aglow,
They trade old jokes, each one a pro.
With every pun, a burst, a squeeze,
They giggle softly, if you please.

The tangy breeze drifts all around,
The laughter echoes, joy is found.
They roll and tumble, what a jest,
It's orange time, let's take a rest.

As night unfolds in starry glee,
The oranges plot what's next, you see.
They'll dream in zest, a nightly jam,
Then wake to dance, oh yes, they can!

The Glow of Grief

A lime once lost, we try to cheer,
"We'll find you soon! Just persevere!"
With citrus valiance, they comb the grove,
In search of zest, we miss the clove.

The tangerines wear frowns so tight,
While grapefruits joke, "We'll be alright!"
In mourning hues, they've donned a cape,
With orange ties, it's no escape.

Yet even grief can take a turn,
As sour notes kick up a churn.
They roast marshmallows, reminisce,
And toast with juice, what a bizarre bliss.

So here we stand with citrus kin,
Through laughter, tears, let love begin.
They glow with warmth, despite the gloom,
In every heart, there's room for bloom.

Citrus Choir

In orchards lush, the fruit unite,
With pitches sweet, they take to flight.
A choir formed of zest and glee,
To sing their songs of jubilee.

The lemons lead, their voices bright,
While limes harmonize through the night.
The oranges join with a joyful shout,
While grapefruits scatter laughs about.

They warble tunes of sunny delight,
With melodies that take to heights.
They juggle jokes like fruit on strings,
In rhythm bound, the laughter rings.

As twilight falls, they raise a cheer,
For citrus gems, so rich and dear.
With every note, they claim the sky,
In joyful chorus, let us fly!

Citrus Colors at Twilight

Lemons laugh in golden rays,
Limes roll down in clumsy ways.
Oranges wink with funny grins,
As tangerines spin round in bins.

Grapefruits dance in evening light,
They juggle jokes, what a sight!
Each fruit a star in twilight's glow,
Their zesty pranks steal the show.

Sweetness in the Breeze

Lemonade whispers in the air,
While limes play tag without a care.
Gusts of joy, they roll and spin,
A fruity circus, let the fun begin!

The wind tugs at orange cheeks,
As playful breezes hide and peek.
The sweetness tickles on the tongue,
Making everyone feel so young.

Groves Beneath a Radiant Sky

Underneath the sun's bright glow,
Silly fruits put up a show.
Grapefruits giggle, tangerines tease,
While lemons dance with utmost ease.

Orange balloons float high and free,
In this grove, it's all silly glee.
With skies so bright, laughs fill the air,
Join the fun, if you dare!

Vibrant Hues of a Juicy Life

In a world of zesty dreams,
Life's as bright as it seems.
With every sip of fruity delight,
We find ourselves lost in the night.

The colors burst, a wild parade,
Lemons in capes, they've got it made.
Oranges are the clowns of the pack,
Squeezing laughs, nothing they lack.

Taste of Serenity

In the orchard where the sun does glow,
Lemons giggle, putting on a show.
Oranges dance, a jolly parade,
Fruit salad dreams in the cool shade.

Lime whispers secrets, oh so sly,
While grapefruit jots down, "Why so shy?"
With zestful leaps and citrus cheer,
Laughter rings out, let's all draw near.

Mandarins joke, bloom after bloom,
Every bite lightens up the room.
Swinging branches, a merry delight,
Here in the grove, everything feels right.

So bring your smiles, take a seat,
Let fruity fun become a treat.
In this grove of blissful mirth,
Juicy joy reigns, a citrus birth.

Vibrant Visions

Sunshine splatters on the garden floor,
A pineapple's laughter, a loud uproar.
Cheeky lemons toss jokes like confetti,
While mandarin mice sneak biscuits, so petty.

Plump grapefruits wear hats—what a sight!
Bouncing off trees, it's pure delight.
Zesty giggles from every vine,
In this vibrant land, all is fine.

The oranges debate, who's the best?
Limes roll their eyes, "Just take a rest!"
Fruitful frolics, leave worries behind,
In this orchard, hilarity's kind.

So dance with the blooms, laugh out loud,
Each citrus slice feels festival proud.
For in this vibrant, fruity display,
Every moment's a silly ballet.

Blossoms & Sunshine

Where blossoms twirl in sunlit air,
Limes jump about without a care.
A banana slips, gives quite a yell,
Citrus giggles—oh, what a swell!

Here, tangerines wear shoes too bright,
Twisting 'round with sheer delight.
Jokes shared 'neath a lemon tree,
Creating laughter, wild and free.

Pomelos smile, spreading good cheer,
As kumquats whisper, "Come over here!"
Zesty parties last through the night,
In this orchard, everything's right.

So come take a stroll through this fun scene,
Where blossoms and sunshine reign supreme.
With each wacky fruit, let joy ignite,
In this grove, where giggles take flight.

Mosaic of Oranges

In a patchwork of orange hues so bright,
Citrus critters prepare for the night.
Dancing lemons on their tiny toes,
Hilarity bubbles, and humor flows.

Peels in the air, a zany display,
Oranges joke, "It's jellybean day!"
With each tangy twist, giggles unite,
In this zesty zone, hearts feel light.

Grapefruits drum on the orchard's beat,
As bananas glide on their fruity feet.
Each vibrant slice enhances the fun,
Under the glow of the setting sun.

So gather 'round for this fruit-inspired spree,
With every laugh, we're wild and free.
In a mosaic of joy, we shall stay,
In this wacky grove, come play, come play!

Sun-Kissed Harvests

In a land where oranges glow bright,
Lemons laugh in the morning light.
Grapefruits roll with a cheeky grin,
Making jests as the day begins.

Frogs in hats skip along the lane,
Dancing while dodging the citrus rain.
The smell of zest fills the warm air,
Squirrels twirl without a care.

Lemonade stands with witty signs,
"Buy one slice, get sunshine as dimes!"
The laughter echoes, it's quite the spree,
In the harvest, joy is the key.

So come gather, join the fun parade,
As we feast on fruit that nature made.
With every laugh and slice we share,
Life's a fruit cocktail beyond compare.

The Tang of Twilight

Underneath the twilight sky,
Limes compete in a sly pie fight.
The tangy zest brings giggles loud,
As the moonbeams join the crowd.

Oranges roll and lemons leap,
While the stars shine bright and deep.
Fruits gossip under the vine,
Whispering secrets, sipping wine.

Mandarins make up new wild games,
While grapefruits take on silly names.
"Citrus Ninja," shouts one with glee,
"Master of the zest!" Oh, what a spree!

When the sun dips low and the fun won't fade,
Nature joins in with its grand parade.
A twilight dance, oh what a sight,
Fruits and laughter under the night.

Citrus Serenade

In the orchard, where laughter sings,
Citrus fruits wear jester's rings.
A serenade of zest and cheer,
With every pluck, there's joy near.

Lemon slices on a sunny plate,
Tell the tale of a silly fate.
They giggle as they spin around,
Their citrusy joy is truly profound.

The oranges dance in a fruity line,
"Who's got the best zest?"—what a fun design!
Apple trees join, in green delight,
As citrus sweetens the cool night.

Puns and laughs mix in the air,
With every citrus, love and care.
So raise a toast to the joy we plant,
In every squeeze, we find our chant.

Squeeze of Sunshine

A sunny morning, bright and bold,
The fruits conspire with tales untold.
A lemon squirted a cheeky grin,
Making all the oranges spin.

"Let's squeeze out the clouds," sang a lime,
"Chasing rainbows is simply sublime!"
The grapefruits joined in the play,
As sunbeams danced the blues away.

With every drop, a giggle rushes,
Through lemon groves and aperitif hushes.
Fruits jump in puddles of sunshine gold,
Leaving behind memories bold.

So let's raise a glass to this funny crew,
For every squeeze shared, there's joy anew.
With every laugh and twist of fate,
Sunshine-filled moments we celebrate!

www.ingramcontent.com/pod-product-compliance
Lightning Source LLC
Chambersburg PA
CBHW060109230426
43661CB00003B/128